DAEWOO DELUXE
Air Fryer Cookbook
FOR UK

Libby Doyle

© Copyright 2022 Libby Doyle - All Rights Reserved.

In no way is it legal to reproduce, duplicate, or transmit any part of this document by either electronic means or in printed format. Recording of this publication is strictly prohibited, and any storage of this material is not allowed unless with written permission from the publisher. All rights reserved.
The information provided herein is stated to be truthful and consistent, in that any liability, regarding inattention or otherwise, by any usage or abuse of any policies, processes, or directions contained within is the solitary and complete responsibility of the recipient reader. Under no circumstances will any legal liability or blame be held against the publisher for any reparation, damages, or monetary loss due to the information herein, either directly or indirectly.
Respective authors own all copyrights not held by the publisher.

Legal Notice:
This book is copyright protected. This is only for personal use. You cannot amend, distribute, sell, use, quote or paraphrase any part of the content within this book without the consent of the author or copyright owner. Legal action will be pursued if this is breached.

Disclaimer Notice:
Please note the information contained within this document is for educational and entertainment purposes only. Every attempt has been made to provide accurate, up-to-date and reliable, complete information. No warranties of any kind are expressed or implied. Readers acknowledge that the author is not engaging in the rendering of legal, financial, medical or professional advice.
By reading this document, the reader agrees that under no circumstances are we responsible for any losses, direct or indirect, which are incurred as a result of the use of information contained within this document, including, but not limited to, errors, omissions, or inaccuracies.

CONTENTS

INTRODUCTION 5
BREAKFAST RECIPES 7

Mixed Peppers Hash	8	Bistro Wedges	17
Potato Rosti	9	Banana Bread	18
Herbed Cheese Balls	10	Lemon Butter Artichokes	19
Mushroom Frittata	11	Bacon and Eggs	19
French Toasts	12	Onion and Cheese Omelet	20
Grilled BBQ Sausages	13	Puffed Egg Tarts	20
Eggs Ramekins	13	Aromatic Potato Hash	21
Egg Baked Omelet	14	Air-Fried Sourdough Sandwiches	22
Cheesy Mustard Toasts	15	Salmon Omelet	22
Cheddar Hash Browns	16		

LUNCH & DINNER RECIPES 23

Fried Pickles	24	Chicken and Asparagus	31
Duck Fat Ribeye	25	Butternut Squash Stew	31
Coconut Tomato	26	Cauliflower Bites	32
Pork and Eggs Bowls	26	Mustard Chicken	33
Pulled Pork	27	Balsamic Cauliflower Stew	33
Lamb and Leeks	27	Rocket Salad	34
Italian Chicken Mix	28	Baby Back Ribs	35
Meatballs	29	Rosemary Lamb	35
Chickpeas	29	Almond Chicken Curry	36
Chicken Quesadillas	30	Seafood Bowls	37

POULTRY RECIPES 38

Easy Turkey Kabobs	39	Fried Chicken Thighs	44
Fennel Chicken	40	Awesome Candied Chicken	44
Dijon-Garlic Thighs	40	Garlicky Meatballs	45
Cheddar Garlic Turkey	41	Appetizing Chicken	46
Cajun Chicken Thighs	41	Herb Chicken Roast	47
Buttered Duck Breasts	42	Agave Mustard Glazed Chicken	48
Buffalo Chicken Strips	42	Herbed Roasted Chicken	49
BBQ Chicken Wings	43		

SNACKS & APPETIZERS RECIPES 50

French Fries	51	Bacon-Wrapped Shrimp	56
Green Bean Crisps	51	Hummus Mushroom Pizza	57
Dad's Boozy Wings	52	Bacon and Onion Fat Bombs	58
Chicken Nuggets	53	Lime Tomato Salsa	58
Cheese Pastries	54	Party Chicken Pillows	59
Cashew Dip	55	Almond Coconut Granola	60
Broccoli Florets	55	Portabella Pizza Treat	61
BBQ Lil Smokies	56		

FISH & SEAFOOD RECIPES 62

Creamy Crab Dip	63	Fijan Coconut Fish	64

Cod with Asparagus 65	Breadcrumbed Fish 70
Coconut Prawns 66	Garlicky Grilled Shrimp 71
Chunky Fish 67	Baked Cod 72
Cheesy Lemon Halibut 68	Herbed Haddock 73
Cajun Spiced Salmon 69	Almond Coconut Shrimp 74
Buttered Scallops 69	Italian Shrimp Scampi 75
Fried Crawfish 70	

VEGETABLE & SIDE DISHES RECIPES 76

Indian Red Potatoes 77	Lemon Asparagus 81
Garlic Broccoli Rabe 78	Balsamic Cabbage Mix 82
Famous Fried Pickles 78	Cheese Zucchini Rolls 82
Dill Tomato 79	Mini Cheese Scones 83
Chives Endives 79	Asian Broccoli 83
Cheese Lings 80	Parmesan Cherry Tomatoes 84
Butter Endives 80	Pop Corn Broccoli 84
Best Roasted Broccoli 81	Air Fried Vegetable Tempura 85

INTRODUCTION

The air fryer is the latest kitchen appliance to sweep America off its feet. The air fryer promises to offer a healthy alternative to the very popular but deeply unhealthy fried food. Most people do not fry at home – with the exception of fried turkey at Thanksgiving – but nevertheless, the air fryer still offers great versatility. By cooking its food at very high temperatures almost immediately, it saves cooks a good deal of time and makes cooking a snap. Let's learn about the air fryer.

HOW AIR FRYERS WORK

An air fryer cooks food by circulating hot air around the food through a traditional convection mechanism. The technology behind the air fryer is nothing exceptionally new. It uses the same process as a convection oven. The hot air is created by a very high-speed fan, which allows for a crispy top layer and tender, juicy interiors. The original air fryer was patented by Turbochef Technologies back in 2005, but its audience was hotel chains and other restaurants.

Phillips introduced its version of the air fryer in 2010 and marketed it to home chefs. The air fryer typically includes a round or egg-shaped fry basket that is easy to clean. Most of the fryer baskets are even dishwasher safe.

IS THE AIR FRYER REALLY HEALTHIER?

According to Phillips, "the air fryer technology results in French fries that includes up to 80% less fat than traditionally-fried foods." But are these kinds of claims really true? According to studies, the answer is a qualified yes.

Deep fryers use about 50 times as much oil as their air frying counterparts. The electric fryer's main health benefit is that it cuts down on the amount of oil absorbed by the food, limiting the overall fat content. Food that is fried in oil is always unhealthy and has a lot of fat calories. A chicken breast that is fried has about 30 percent more fat than roasted chicken. An air fryer will not necessarily cook chicken healthier than baking it in an oven, but it will produce the crispy skin that people love in fried chicken.

Another benefit of an air fryer is avoiding the bad compounds which develop during the oil frying process. One of the compounds, acrylamide, may be linked to several cancers, including pancreatic, breast and ovarian cancer. The compound is created during high-heat cooking with oil. This compound does not form during the air frying process.

A study of the characteristics of French fries produced by deep fat frying and air frying found that the air fryer potatoes tasted like traditional French fries but with a substantially lower level of fat absorbed in the product. Again, this is due to the small amount of oil used in the air fryer.

However, you should not cook all of your foods in an air fryer, since air fryers still fry food. Fried foods are linked to heart conditions, high blood pressure, diabetes and some cancers. Limiting fried foods and focusing on healthy cooking methods such as roasting, steaming and sauteing are still best for daily cooking.

Breakfast Recipes

Mixed Peppers Hash

Ingredients:

- 1 red bell pepper, cut into strips
- 1 green bell pepper, cut into strips
- 1 orange bell pepper, cut into strips
- 4 eggs, whisked
- Salt and black pepper to the taste
- 2 tablespoons mozzarella, shredded
- Cooking spray

Servings: 4
Cooking Time: 20 minutes

Directions:

1. In a bowl, mix the eggs with all the bell peppers, salt and pepper and toss. Preheat the air fryer at 350 degrees F, grease it with cooking spray, pour the eggs mixture, spread well, sprinkle the mozzarella on top and cook for 20 minutes.
2. Divide between plates and serve for breakfast.

Potato Rosti

Ingredients:

- 1 teaspoon olive oil
- ½ pound russet potatoes, peeled and roughly grated
- 1 tablespoon fresh chives, finely chopped
- Salt and ground black pepper, as required
- 2 tablespoons sour cream
- 3½ ounces smoked salmon, cut into slices

Servings: 2
Cooking Time: 15 minutes

Directions:

1. Set the temperature of Air Fryer to 355 degrees F. Grease a pizza pan with the olive oil.
2. In a large bowl, mix together the potatoes, chives, salt, and black pepper.
3. Place the potato mixture into the prepared pizza pan.
4. Arrange the pan in an Air Fryer basket.
5. Air Fry for about 15 minutes or until the top becomes golden brown.
6. Cut the potato rosti into wedges.
7. Top with the sour cream and smoked salmon slices and serve immediately.

Herbed Cheese Balls

Servings: 3
Cooking Time: 9 minutes

Ingredients:

- 1 teaspoon garlic powder
- 1 oz Parmesan, grated
- ½ cup Cheddar cheese, shredded
- 1 egg, beaten
- 1 tablespoon cream cheese
- 1 teaspoon dried dill
- 1 teaspoon dried cilantro
- 1 teaspoon dried parsley
- Cooking spray

Directions:

1. Mix up Parmesan and Cheddar cheese. Add garlic powder, egg, cream cheese, dried dill, cilantro, and parsley. Stir the mixture until homogenous. With the help of the scoop make the cheese balls and put them in the freezer for 15 minutes. Preheat the air fryer to 400F.
2. Then spray the air fryer basket with cooking spray. Put the frozen cheese balls in the air fryer basket. Cook them for 9 minutes or until they are golden brown.

Mushroom Frittata

Ingredients:

- 1 cup egg whites
- 1 cup spinach, chopped
- 2 mushrooms, sliced
- 2 tbsp parmesan cheese, grated
- Salt

Servings: 1
Cooking Time: 13 minutes

Directions:

1. Spray pan with cooking spray and heat over medium heat.
2. Add mushrooms and sauté for 2-3 minutes. Add spinach and cook for 1-2 minutes or until wilted.
3. Transfer mushroom spinach mixture into the air fryer pan.
4. Whisk egg whites in a mixing bowl until frothy. Season with a pinch of salt.
5. Pour egg white mixture into the spinach and mushroom mixture and sprinkle with parmesan cheese.
6. Place pan in air fryer basket and cook frittata at 350 F for 8 minutes.
7. Slice and serve.

French Toasts

Servings: 2
Cooking Time: 3 minutes

Ingredients:

- 2 eggs
- ¼ cup evaporated milk
- 3 tablespoons sugar
- 2 teaspoons olive oil
- 1/8 teaspoon vanilla extract
- 4 bread slices

Directions:

1. Set the temperature of Air Fryer to 390 degrees F. Grease an Air Fryer pan and insert in the Air Fryer while heating.
2. In a large bowl, mix together all the above ingredients except bread slices.
3. Coat the bread slices evenly with egg mixture.
4. Arrange the bread slices in the prepared pan.
5. Air Fry for about 2-3 minutes per side.
6. Serve warm.

Grilled BBQ Sausages

Ingredients:
- 6 sausage links
- ½ cup prepared BBQ sauce

Directions:
1. Preheat the air fryer at 3900F.
2. Place the grill pan accessory in the air fryer.
3. Place the sausage links and grill for 30 minutes.
4. Flip halfway through the cooking time.
5. Before serving brush with prepared BBQ sauce.

Servings: 3
Cooking Time: 30 minutes

Eggs Ramekins

Ingredients:
- 5 eggs
- 1 teaspoon coconut oil, melted
- ¼ teaspoon ground black pepper

Directions:
1. Brush the ramekins with coconut oil and crack the eggs inside. Then sprinkle the eggs with ground black pepper and transfer in the air fryer. Cook the baked eggs for 6 minutes at 355F.

Servings: 5
Cooking Time: 6 minutes

Egg Baked Omelet

Ingredients:

- tbsp. ricotta cheese
- 1 tbsp. chopped parsley
- 1 tsp. olive oil
- 3 eggs
- ¼ cup chopped spinach
- Salt and pepper to taste

Servings: 1
Cooking Time: 15 minutes

Directions:

1. Set your Air Fryer at 330°F and allow to warm with the olive oil inside.
2. In a bowl, beat the eggs with a fork and sprinkle some salt and pepper as desired.
3. Add in the ricotta, spinach, and parsley and then transfer to the Air Fryer. Cook for 10 minutes before serving.

Cheesy Mustard Toasts

Ingredients:
- 4 bread slices
- 2 tablespoons cheddar cheese, shredded
- 2 eggs, whites and yolks, separated
- 1 tablespoon mustard
- 1 tablespoon paprika

Directions:
1. Set the temperature of Air Fryer to 355 degrees F.
2. Place the bread slices in an Air fryer basket.
3. Air Fry for about 5 minutes or until toasted.
4. Add the egg whites in a clean glass bowl and beat until they form soft peaks.
5. In another bowl, mix together the cheese, egg yolks, mustard, and paprika.
6. Gently, fold in the egg whites.
7. Spread the mustard mixture over the toasted bread slices.
8. Air Fry for about 10 minutes.
9. Serve warm!

Servings: 4
Cooking Time: 15 minutes

Cheddar Hash Browns

Ingredients:

- 1 brown onion, chopped
- 3 garlic cloves, chopped
- ½ cup grated cheddar cheese
- 1 egg, lightly beaten
- Salt and black pepper
- 3 tbsp finely thyme sprigs
- Cooking spray

Servings: 4
Cooking Time: 25 minutes

Directions:

1. In a bowl, mix with hands potatoes, onion, garlic, cheese, egg, salt, black pepper, and thyme. Spray the fryer with cooking spray.
2. Press the hash brown mixture into the basket and cook for 9 minutes at 400 F., shaking once halfway through cooking. When ready, ensure the hash browns are golden and crispy.

Bistro Wedges

Servings: 4
Cooking Time: 20 minutes

Ingredients:

- 1 lb. fingerling potatoes, cut into wedges
- 1 tsp. extra virgin olive oil
- ½ tsp. garlic powder
- Salt and pepper to taste
- ½ cup raw cashews, soaked in water overnight
- ½ tsp. ground turmeric
- ½ tsp. paprika
- 1 tbsp. nutritional yeast
- 1 tsp. fresh lemon juice
- 2 tbsp. to ¼ cup water

Directions:

1. Pre-heat your Air Fryer at 400°F.
2. In a bowl, toss together the potato wedges, olive oil, garlic powder, and salt and pepper, making sure to coat the potatoes well.
3. Transfer the potatoes to the basket of your fryer and fry for 10 minutes.
4. In the meantime, prepare the cheese sauce. Pulse the cashews, turmeric, paprika, nutritional yeast, lemon juice, and water together in a food processor. Add more water to achieve your desired consistency.
5. When the potatoes are finished cooking, move them to a bowl that is small enough to fit inside the fryer and add the cheese sauce on top. Cook for an additional 3 minutes.

Banana Bread

Ingredients:

- 1 1/3 cups flour
- 1 teaspoon baking soda
- 1 teaspoon baking powder
- ½ cup milk
- 3 bananas, peeled and sliced
- 2/3 cup sugar
- 1 teaspoon ground cinnamon
- 1 teaspoon salt
- ½ cup olive oil

Servings: 8
Cooking Time: 20 minutes

Directions:

1. Preheat the Air fryer to 330 o F and grease a loaf pan.
2. Mix together all the dry ingredients with the wet ingredients to form a dough.
3. Place the dough into the prepared loaf pan and transfer into an air fryer basket.
4. Cook for about 20 minutes and remove from air fryer.
5. Cut the bread into desired size slices and serve warm.

Lemon Butter Artichokes

Ingredients:

- 2 medium artichokes, trimmed and halved
- 2 tbsp fresh lemon juice
- 1 tbsp butter, melted
- Pepper
- Salt

Servings: 4
Cooking Time: 15 minutes

Directions:

1. Place artichokes into the air fryer basket. Drizzle with butter and lemon juice and season with pepper and salt.
2. Cook at 380 F for 15 minutes.
3. Serve and enjoy.

Bacon and Eggs

Ingredients:

- Parsley
- Cherry tomatoes
- 1/3 oz/150g bacon
- eggs

Servings: 4
Cooking Time: 15 minutes

Directions:

1. Fry up the bacon and put it to the side.
2. Scramble the eggs in the bacon grease, with some pepper and salt. If you want, scramble in some cherry tomatoes. Sprinkle with some parsley and enjoy.

Onion and Cheese Omelet

Servings: 1
Cooking Time: 15 minutes

Ingredients:

- 2 tbsp grated cheddar cheese
- 1 tsp soy sauce
- ½ onion, sliced
- ¼ tsp pepper
- 1 tbsp olive oil

Directions:

1. Whisk the eggs along with the pepper and soy sauce. Preheat the air fryer to 350 F. Heat the olive oil and add the egg mixture and the onion. Cook for 8 to 10 minutes. Top with the grated cheddar cheese.

Puffed Egg Tarts

Servings: 4
Cooking Time: 42 minutes

Ingredients:

- 1 sheet frozen puff pastry half, thawed and cut into 4 squares
- ¾ cup Monterey Jack cheese, shredded and divided
- 4 large eggs
- 1 tablespoon fresh parsley, minced
- 1 tablespoon olive oil

Directions:

1. Preheat the Air fryer to 390 o F
2. Place 2 pastry squares in the air fryer basket and cook for about 10 minutes.
3. Remove Air fryer basket from the Air fryer and press each square gently with a metal tablespoon to form an indentation.
4. Place 3 tablespoons of cheese in each hole and top with 1 egg each.
5. Return Air fryer basket to Air fryer and cook for about 11 minutes.
6. Remove tarts from the Air fryer basket and sprinkle with half the parsley.
7. Repeat with remaining pastry squares, cheese and eggs.
8. Dish out and serve warm.

Aromatic Potato Hash

Servings: 4
Cooking Time: 42 minutes

Ingredients:

- 2 teaspoons butter, melted
- 1 medium onion, chopped
- ½ of green bell pepper, seeded and chopped
- 1½ pound russet potatoes, peeled and cubed
- 5 eggs, beaten
- ½ teaspoon dried thyme, crushed
- ½ teaspoon dried savory, crushed
- Salt and black pepper, to taste

Directions:

1. Preheat the Air fryer to 390 o F and grease an Air fryer pan with melted butter.
2. Put onion and bell pepper in the Air fryer pan and cook for about 5 minutes.
3. Add the potatoes, thyme, savory, salt and black pepper and cook for about 30 minutes.
4. Meanwhile, heat a greased skillet on medium heat and stir in the beaten eggs.
5. Cook for about 1 minute on each side and remove from the skillet.
6. Cut it into small pieces and transfer the egg pieces into the Air fryer pan.
7. Cook for about 5 more minutes and serve warm.

Air-Fried Sourdough Sandwiches

Servings: 2
Cooking Time: 25 minutes

Ingredients:
- 2 tbsp mayonnaise
- 2 slices ham
- 2 lettuce leaves
- 1 tomato, sliced
- 2 slices mozzarella cheese
- Salt and pepper to taste
- Cooking spray

Directions:
1. On a clean board, lay the sourdough slices and spread with mayonnaise. Top 2 of the slices with ham, lettuce, tomato, and mozzarella cheese. Season with salt and pepper.
2. Top with the remaining two slices to form two sandwiches. Spray with oil and transfer to the air fryer. Cook for 14 minutes at 340 F, flipping once halfway through cooking. Serve hot!

Salmon Omelet

Servings: 2
Cooking Time: 15 minutes

Ingredients:
- 3 eggs
- 1 smoked salmon
- 3 links pork sausage
- ¼ cup onions
- ¼ cup provolone cheese

Directions:
1. Whisk the eggs and pour them into a skillet.
2. Follow the standard method for making an omelette.
3. Add the onions, salmon and cheese before turning the omelet over.
4. Sprinkle the omelet with cheese and serve with the sausages on the side.
5. Serve!

Lunch & Dinner Recipes

Fried Pickles

Ingredients:

- 14 dill pickles, sliced
- ¼ cup flour
- 1/8 tsp. baking powder
- Pinch of salt
- 2 tbsp. cornstarch + 3 tbsp. water
- 6 tbsp. bread crumbs
- ½ tsp. paprika
- Cooking spray

Servings: 4
Cooking Time: 30 minutes

Directions:

1. Pre-heat your Air Fryer at 400°F.
2. Drain any excess moisture out of the dill pickles on a paper towel.
3. In a bowl, combine the flour, baking powder and salt.
4. Throw in the cornstarch and water mixture and combine well with a whisk.
5. Put the panko bread crumbs in a shallow dish along with the paprika. Mix thoroughly.
6. Dip the pickles in the flour batter, before coating in the bread crumbs. Spritz all the pickles with the cooking spray.
7. Transfer to the fryer and cook for 15 minutes, until a golden brown color is achieved.

Duck Fat Ribeye

Ingredients:

- One 16-oz ribeye steak (1 - 1 ¼ inch thick)
- 1 tbsp duck fat (or other high smoke point oil like peanut oil)
- ½ tbsp butter
- ½ tsp thyme, chopped
- Salt and pepper to taste

Servings: 1
Cooking Time: 20 minutes

Directions:

1. Preheat a skillet in your fryer at 400°F/200°C.
2. Season the steaks with the oil, salt and pepper. Remove the skillet from the fryer once pre-heated.
3. Put the skillet on your stove top burner on a medium heat and drizzle in the oil.
4. Sear the steak for 1-4 minutes, depending on if you like it rare, medium or well done.
5. Turn over the steak and place in your fryer for 6 minutes.
6. Take out the steak from your fryer and place it back on the stove top on low heat.
7. Toss in the butter and thyme and cook for 3 minutes, basting as you go along.
8. Rest for 5 minutes and serve.

Coconut Tomato

Ingredients:
- 1/3 cup coconut cream
- ½ pound cherry tomatoes, halved
- 2 avocados, pitted, peeled and cubed
- A pinch of salt and black pepper
- Cooking spray

Servings: 4
Cooking Time: 5 minutes

Directions:
1. Grease the air fryer with cooking spray, combine the tomatoes with avocados, and the other ingredients and cook at 350 degrees F for 5 minutes shaking once. Divide into bowls and serve

Pork and Eggs Bowls

Ingredients:
- 2 eggs, whisked
- 1 and ½ pounds pork meat, ground
- 2 teaspoons olive oil
- ½ cup keto tomato sauce
- Salt and black pepper to the taste

Servings: 4
Cooking Time: 15 minutes

Directions:
1. Heat up a pan that fits the Air Fryer with the oil over medium-high heat, add the meat and brown for 3-4 minutes.
2. Add the rest of the ingredients, toss, put the pan in the machine and cook at 370 degrees F for 12 minutes. Divide into bowls and serve for lunch with a side salad.

Pulled Pork

Ingredients:
- 1 lb. pork tenderloin
- 2 tbsp. barbecue dry rub
- 1/3 cup heavy cream
- 1 tsp. butter

Servings: 1
Cooking Time: 30 minutes

Directions:
1. Pre-heat your fryer at 370°F.
2. Massage the dry rub of your choice into the tenderloin, coating it well.
3. Cook the tenderloin in the fryer for twenty minutes. When cooked, shred with two forks.
4. Add the heavy cream and butter into the fryer along with the shredded pork and stir well. Cook for a further four minutes.
5. Allow to cool a little, then serve and enjoy.

Lamb and Leeks

Ingredients:
- 1 pound lamb shoulder, trimmed and cubed
- 2 tablespoons olive oil
- 3 garlic cloves, minced
- 4 baby leeks, halved
- 1 cup okra
- 1 pound tomatoes, peeled and chopped
- Salt and black pepper to the taste
- 2 tablespoons tarragon, chopped

Servings: 4
Cooking Time: 30 minutes

Directions:
1. Heat up a pan that fits your air fryer with the oil over medium-high heat, add the lamb, garlic, salt and pepper, toss and brown for 5 minutes.
2. Add the remaining ingredients except the tarragon, toss, introduce the pan in the fryer and cook at 400 degrees F for 25 minutes. Divide everything into bowls and serve for lunch.

Italian Chicken Mix

Servings: 4
Cooking Time: 20 minutes

Ingredients:

- 1 cup chicken stock
- Salt and black pepper to taste
- 8 chicken drumsticks, bone-in
- 1 teaspoon garlic powder
- 1 yellow onion, chopped
- 28 ounces canned tomatoes, chopped
- 1 teaspoon oregano, dried
- ½ cup black olives, pitted and sliced

Directions:

1. Add all the ingredients to a baking dish that fits your air fryer and toss.
2. Place the dish in your air fryer and cook at 380 degrees F for 20 minutes.
3. Divide the mix into bowls and serve.

Meatballs

Ingredients:

- 1 lb ground beef (or ½ lb beef, ½ lb pork)
- ½ cup grated parmesan cheese
- 1 tbsp minced garlic (or paste)
- ½ cup mozzarella cheese
- 1 tsp freshly ground pepper

Directions:

1. Preheat your fryer to 400°F/200°C.
2. In a bowl, mix all the ingredients together.
3. Roll the meat mixture into 5 generous meatballs.
4. Bake inside your fryer at 170°F/80°C for about 18 minutes.
5. Serve with sauce!

Servings: 6
Cooking Time: 30 minutes

Chickpeas

Ingredients:

- 1 15-oz. can chickpeas, drained but not rinsed
- 2 tbsp. olive oil
- 1 tsp. salt
- 2 tbsp. lemon juice

Directions:

1. Pre-heat the Air Fryer at 400°F.
2. Add all the ingredients together in a bowl and mix. Transfer this mixture to the basket of the fryer.
3. Cook for 15 minutes, ensuring the chickpeas become nice and crispy.

Servings: 4
Cooking Time: 20 minutes

Chicken Quesadillas

Ingredients:

- 2 soft taco shells
- 1 lb. boneless chicken breasts
- 1 large green pepper, sliced
- 1 medium-sized onion, sliced
- ½ cup Cheddar cheese, shredded
- ½ cup salsa sauce
- 2 tbsp. olive oil
- Salt and pepper, to taste

Servings: 4
Cooking Time: 20 minutes

Directions:

1. Pre-heat the Air Fryer to 370°F and drizzle the basket with 1 tablespoon of olive oil.
2. Lay one taco shell into the bottom of the fryer and spread some salsa inside the taco. Slice the chicken breast into strips and put the strips into taco shell.
3. Top the chicken with the onions and peppers.
4. Season with salt and pepper. Add the shredded cheese and top with the second taco shell.
5. Drizzle with another tablespoon of olive oil. Put the rack over the taco to keep it in place.
6. Cook for 4 – 6 minutes, until it turns lightly brown and is cooked through. Serve either hot or cold.

Chicken and Asparagus

Ingredients:

- 4 chicken breasts, skinless, boneless and halved
- 1 tablespoon sweet paprika
- 1 bunch asparagus, trimmed and halved
- 1 tablespoon olive oil
- Salt and black pepper to the taste

Servings: 4
Cooking Time: 20 minutes

Directions:

1. In a bowl, mix all the ingredients, toss, put them in your Air Fryer's basket and cook at 390 degrees F for 20 minutes. Divide between plates and serve for lunch.

Butternut Squash Stew

Ingredients:

- 1½ pounds butternut squash, cubed
- ½ cup green onions, chopped
- 3 tablespoons butter, melted
- ½ cup carrots, chopped
- ½ cup celery, chopped
- 1 garlic clove, minced
- ½ teaspoon Italian seasoning
- 15 ounces canned tomatoes, chopped
- Salt and black pepper to taste
- ⅛ teaspoon red pepper flakes, dried
- 1 cup quinoa, cooked
- 1½ cups heavy cream
- 1 cup chicken meat, already cooked and shredded

Servings: 5
Cooking Time: 15 minutes

Directions:

1. Place all the ingredients in a pan that fits your air fryer and toss.
2. Put the pan into the fryer and cook at 400 degrees F for 15 minutes.
3. Divide the stew between bowls, serve, and enjoy.

Cauliflower Bites

Servings: 4
Cooking Time: 30 minutes

Ingredients:

- 1 cup flour
- ⅓ cup desiccated coconut
- Salt and pepper to taste
- 1 flax egg [1 tbsp. flaxseed meal + 3 tbsp. water]
- 1 small cauliflower, cut into florets
- 1 tsp. mixed spice
- ½ tsp. mustard powder
- 2 tbsp. maple syrup
- 1 clove of garlic, minced
- 2 tbsp. soy sauce

Directions:

1. Pre-heat the Air Fryer to 400°F.
2. In a bowl, mix together the oats, flour, and desiccated coconut, sprinkling with some salt and pepper as desired.
3. In a separate bowl, season the flax egg with a pinch of salt.
4. Coat the cauliflower with mixed spice and mustard powder.
5. Dip the florets into the flax egg, then into the flour mixture. Cook for 15 minutes in the fryer.
6. In the meantime, place a saucepan over medium heat and add in the maple syrup, garlic, and soy sauce. Boil first, before reducing the heat to allow the sauce to thicken.
7. Remove the florets from the Air Fryer and transfer to the saucepan. Coat the florets in the sauce before returning to the fryer and allowing to cook for an additional 5 minutes.

Mustard Chicken

Ingredients:

- 1 and ½ pounds chicken thighs, bone-in
- 2 tablespoons Dijon mustard
- A pinch of salt and black pepper
- Cooking spray

Servings: 4
Cooking Time: 30 minutes

Directions:

1. In a bowl, mix the chicken thighs with all the other ingredients and toss. Put the chicken in your Air Fryer's basket and cook at 370 degrees F for 30 minutes shaking halfway. Serve these chicken thighs for lunch.

Balsamic Cauliflower Stew

Ingredients:

- 1 and ½ cups zucchinis, sliced
- 1 tablespoon olive oil
- Salt and black pepper to the taste
- 1 tablespoon balsamic vinegar
- 1 cauliflower head, florets separated
- 2 green onions, chopped
- 1 handful parsley leaves, chopped
- ½ cup keto tomato sauce

Servings: 4
Cooking Time: 20 minutes

Directions:

1. In a pan that fits your air fryer, mix the zucchinis with the rest of the ingredients except the parsley, toss, introduce the pan in the air fryer and cook at 380 degrees F for 20 minutes.
2. Divide into bowls and serve for lunch with parsley sprinkled on top.

Rocket Salad

Ingredients:

- 8 fresh figs, halved
- 1 ½ cups chickpeas, cooked
- 1 tsp. cumin seeds, roasted then crushed
- 4 tbsp. balsamic vinegar
- 2 tbsp. extra-virgin olive oil
- Salt and pepper to taste
- 3 cups arugula rocket, washed and dried

Servings: 4
Cooking Time: 35 minutes

Directions:

1. Pre-heat the Air Fryer to 375°F.
2. Cover the Air Fryer basket with aluminum foil and grease lightly with oil. Put the figs in the fryer and allow to cook for 10 minutes.
3. In a bowl, combine the chickpeas and cumin seeds.
4. Remove the cooked figs from the fryer and replace with chickpeas. Cook for 10 minutes. Leave to cool.
5. In the meantime, prepare the dressing. Mix together the balsamic vinegar, olive oil, salt and pepper.
6. In a salad bowl combine the arugula rocket with the cooled figs and chickpeas.
7. Toss with the sauce and serve right away.

Baby Back Ribs

Ingredients:

- 2 tsp. red pepper flakes
- ¾ ground ginger
- 3 cloves minced garlic
- Salt and pepper
- 2 baby back ribs

Servings: 2
Cooking Time: 45 minutes

Directions:

1. Pre-heat your fryer at 350°F.
2. Combine the red pepper flakes, ginger, garlic, salt and pepper in a bowl, making sure to mix well. Massage the mixture into the baby back ribs.
3. Cook the ribs in the fryer for thirty minutes.
4. Take care when taking the rubs out of the fryer. Place them on a serving dish and enjoy with a low-carb barbecue sauce of your choosing.

Rosemary Lamb

Ingredients:

- 1 tablespoon olive oil
- 2 garlic clove, minced
- 1 tablespoon rosemary, chopped
- ¼ cup keto tomato sauce
- 1 cup baby spinach
- 1 and ½ pounds lamb, cubed
- Salt and black pepper to the taste

Servings: 4
Cooking Time: 30 minutes

Directions:

1. Heat up a pan that fits the air fryer with the oil over medium heat, add the lamb and garlic and brown for 5 minutes. Add the rest of the ingredients except the spinach, introduce the pan in the fryer and cook at 390 degrees F for 15 minutes, shaking the machine halfway.
2. Add the spinach, cook for 10 minutes more, divide between plates and serve for lunch.

Almond Chicken Curry

Servings: 2
Cooking Time: 15 minutes

Ingredients:

- 10 oz chicken fillet, chopped
- 1 teaspoon ground turmeric
- ½ cup spring onions, diced
- 1 teaspoon salt
- ½ teaspoon curry powder
- ½ teaspoon garlic, diced
- ½ teaspoon ground coriander
- ½ cup of organic almond milk
- 1 teaspoon Truvia
- 1 teaspoon olive oil

Directions:

1. Put the chicken in the bowl. Add the ground turmeric, salt, curry powder, diced garlic, ground coriander, and almond Truvia. Then add olive oil and mix up the chicken. After this, add almond milk and transfer the chicken in the air fryer pan. Then preheat the air fryer to 375F and place the pan with korma curry inside.
2. Top the chicken with diced onion. Cook the meal for 10 minutes. Stir it after 5 minutes of cooking. If the chicken is not cooked after 10 minutes, cook it for an additional 5 minutes.

Seafood Bowls

Ingredients:

- 2 salmon fillets, boneless, skinless and cubed
- 8 ounces shrimp, peeled and deveined
- Salt and black pepper to the taste
- 5 garlic cloves, minced
- 1 teaspoon sweet paprika
- 2 tablespoons olive oil

Servings: 4
Cooking Time: 12 minutes

Directions:

1. In a pan that fits the air fryer, combine all the ingredients, toss, cover and cook at 370 degrees F for 12 minutes. Divide into bowls and serve for lunch.

Poultry Recipes

Easy Turkey Kabobs

Ingredients:

- 1 cup parmesan cheese, grated
- 1 ½ cups of water
- 14 ounces ground turkey
- 2 small eggs, beaten
- 1 teaspoon ground ginger
- 2 ½ tablespoons vegetable oil
- 1 cup chopped fresh parsley
- 2 tablespoons almond meal
- 3/4 teaspoon salt
- 1 heaping teaspoon fresh rosemary, finely chopped
- 1/2 teaspoon ground allspice

Servings: 8
Cooking Time: 15 minutes

Directions:

1. Mix all of the above ingredients in a bowl. Knead the mixture with your hands.
2. Then, take small portions and gently roll them into balls.
3. Now, preheat your Air Fryer to 380 degrees F. Air fry for 8 to 10 minutes in the Air Fryer basket. Serve on a serving platter with skewers and eat with your favorite dipping sauce.

Fennel Chicken

Ingredients:

- 1 ½ cup coconut milk
- 2 tbsp. garam masala
- 1 ½ lb. chicken thighs
- ¾ tbsp. coconut oil, melted

Servings: 4
Cooking Time: 40 minutes

Directions:

1. Combine the coconut oil and garam masala together in a bowl. Pour the mixture over the chicken thighs and leave to marinate for a half hour.
2. Pre-heat your fryer at 375°F.
3. Cook the chicken into the fryer for fifteen minutes.
4. Add in the coconut milk, giving it a good stir, then cook for an additional ten minutes.
5. Remove the chicken and place on a serving dish. Make sure to pour all of the coconut "gravy" over it and serve immediately.

Dijon-Garlic Thighs

Ingredients:

- 1 tablespoon cider vinegar
- 1 tablespoon Dijon mustard
- 1-pound chicken thighs
- 2 tablespoon olive oil
- 2 teaspoons herbs de Provence
- Salt and pepper to taste

Servings: 6
Cooking Time: 25 minutes

Directions:

1. Place all ingredients in a Ziploc bag.
2. Allow to marinate in the fridge for at least 2 hours.
3. Preheat the air fryer for 5 minutes.
4. Place the chicken in the fryer basket.
5. Cook for 25 minutes at 3500F.

Cheddar Garlic Turkey

Ingredients:

- 1 big turkey breast, skinless, boneless and cubed
- Salt and black pepper to the taste
- ¼ cup cheddar cheese, grated
- ¼ teaspoon garlic powder
- 1 tablespoon olive oil

Servings: 4
Cooking Time: 20 minutes

Directions:

1. Rub the turkey cubes with the oil, season with salt, pepper and garlic powder and dredge in cheddar cheese. Put the turkey bits in your air fryer's basket and cook at 380 degrees F for 20 minutes.
2. Divide between plates and serve with a side salad.

Cajun Chicken Thighs

Ingredients:

- ½ cup all-purpose flour
- 1 egg
- 4 (4-ounces) skin-on chicken thighs
- 1½ tablespoons Cajun seasoning
- 1 teaspoon seasoning salt

Servings: 4
Cooking Time: 25 minutes

Directions:

1. Preheat the Air fryer to 355 o F and grease an Air fryer basket.
2. Mix the flour, Cajun seasoning and salt in a bowl.
3. Whisk the egg in another bowl and coat the chicken thighs with the flour mixture.
4. Dip into the egg and dredge again into the flour mixture.
5. Arrange the chicken thighs into the Air Fryer basket, skin side down and cook for about 25 minutes.
6. Dish out the chicken thighs onto a serving platter and serve hot.

Buttered Duck Breasts

Ingredients:
- 2 (12-ounces) duck breasts
- 3 tablespoons unsalted butter, melted
- Salt and ground black pepper, as required
- ½ teaspoon dried thyme, crushed
- ¼ teaspoon star anise powder

Directions:
1. Preheat the Air fryer to 390 o F and grease an Air fryer basket.
2. Season the duck breasts generously with salt and black pepper.
3. Arrange the duck breasts into the prepared Air fryer basket and cook for about 10 minutes.
4. Dish out the duck breasts and drizzle with melted butter.
5. Season with thyme and star anise powder and place the duck breasts again into the Air fryer basket.
6. Cook for about 12 more minutes and dish out to serve warm.

Servings: 4
Cooking Time: 22 minutes

Buffalo Chicken Strips

Ingredients:
- ¼ cup hot sauce
- 1 lb. boneless skinless chicken tenders
- 1 tsp. garlic powder
- 1 ½ oz. pork rinds, finely ground
- 1 tsp chili powder

Directions:
1. Toss the hot sauce and chicken tenders together in a bowl, ensuring the chicken is completely coated.
2. In another bowl, combine the garlic powder, ground pork rinds, and chili powder. Use this mixture to coat the tenders, covering them well. Place the chicken into your fryer, taking care not to layer pieces on top of one another.
3. Cook the chicken at 375°F for twenty minutes until cooked all the way through and golden. Serve warm with your favorite dips and sides.

Servings: 1
Cooking Time: 30 minutes

BBQ Chicken Wings

Ingredients:

- 1 1/2 lbs chicken wings
- 2 tbsp unsweetened BBQ sauce
- 1 tsp paprika
- 1 tbsp olive oil
- 1 tsp garlic powder
- Pepper
- Salt

Servings: 4
Cooking Time: 20 minutes

Directions:

1. In a large bowl, toss chicken wings with garlic powder, oil, paprika, pepper, and salt.
2. Preheat the air fryer to 360 F.
3. Add chicken wings in air fryer basket and cook for 12 minutes.
4. Turn chicken wings to another side and cook for 5 minutes more.
5. Remove chicken wings from air fryer and toss with BBQ sauce.
6. Return chicken wings in air fryer basket and cook for 2 minutes more.
7. Serve and enjoy.

Fried Chicken Thighs

Ingredients:

- 4 chicken thighs
- 1 ½ tbsp. Cajun seasoning
- 1 egg, beaten
- ½ cup flour
- 1 tsp. seasoning salt

Servings: 4
Cooking Time: 35 minutes

Directions:

1. Pre-heat the Air Fryer to 350°F.
2. In a bowl combine the flour, Cajun seasoning, and seasoning salt.
3. Place the beaten egg in another bowl.
4. Coat the chicken with the flour before dredging it in the egg. Roll once more in the flour.
5. Put the chicken in the Air Fryer and cook for 25 minutes. Serve hot.

Awesome Candied Chicken

Ingredients:

- ½ tbsp flour
- 5 chicken breasts, sliced
- 1 tbsp Worcestershire sauce
- 3 tbsp olive oil
- ¼ cup onions, chopped
- 1 ½ cups brown sugar
- ¼ cup yellow mustard
- ¾ cup water
- ½ cup ketchup

Servings: 6
Cooking Time: 20 minutes

Directions:

1. Preheat your Fryer to 360 F. In a bowl, mix in flour, salt and pepper. Cover the chicken slices with flour mixture and drizzle oil over the chicken. In another bowl, mix brown sugar, water, ketchup, chopped onion, mustard, Worcestershire sauce and salt. Transfer chicken to marinade mixture; set aside for 10 minutes.
2. Place the chicken in your air fryer's cooking basket and cook for 15 minutes.

Garlicky Meatballs

Ingredients:
- ½ lb. boneless chicken thighs
- 1 tsp. minced garlic
- 1 ¼ cup roasted pecans
- ½ cup mushrooms
- 1 tsp. extra virgin olive oil

Servings: 2
Cooking Time: 20 minutes

Directions:
1. Preheat your fryer to 375°F.
2. Cube the chicken thighs.
3. Place them in the food processor along with the garlic, pecans, and other seasonings as desired. Pulse until a smooth consistency is achieved.
4. Chop the mushrooms finely. Add to the chicken mixture and combine.
5. Using your hands, shape the mixture into balls and brush them with olive oil.
6. Put the balls into the fryer and cook for eighteen minutes. Serve hot.

Appetizing Chicken

Servings: 2
Cooking Time: 19 minutes

Ingredients:

- ¾ pound chicken pieces
- 1 tablespoon fresh rosemary, chopped
- 1 lemon, cut into wedges
- 1 teaspoon ginger, minced
- 1 tablespoon soy sauce
- ½ tablespoon olive oil
- 1 tablespoon oyster sauce
- 3 tablespoons brown sugar

Directions:

1. Preheat the Air fryer to 390 o F and grease an Air fryer basket.
2. Mix chicken, ginger, soy sauce and olive oil in a bowl.
3. Marinate and refrigerate for about 30 minutes and transfer the chicken in the Air fryer pan.
4. Cook for about 6 minutes and dish out.
5. Meanwhile, mix the remaining ingredients in a small bowl and spread over the chicken.
6. Squeeze juice from lemon wedges over chicken and top with the wedges.
7. Transfer into the Air fryer and cook for about 13 minutes.
8. Dish out and serve warm.

Herb Chicken Roast

Ingredients:

- 10 oz chicken breast
- 1/4 tsp dried thyme
- 1/2 tsp paprika
- 1 tbsp butter
- 1/4 tsp black pepper
- 1/4 tsp garlic powder
- 1/4 tsp dried rosemary
- 1/4 tsp salt

Servings: 2
Cooking Time: 25 minutes

Directions:

1. In a small bowl, combine together butter, black pepper, garlic powder, rosemary, thyme, paprika, and salt.
2. Rub chicken with butter spice herb mixture and place into the air fryer basket.
3. Cook at 375 F for 25 minutes.
4. Serve and enjoy.

Agave Mustard Glazed Chicken

Ingredients:

- 1 tablespoon avocado oil
- 2 pounds chicken breasts, boneless, skin-on
- 1 tablespoon Jamaican Jerk Rub
- 1/2 teaspoon salt
- 3 tablespoons agave syrup
- 1 tablespoon mustard
- 2 tablespoons scallions, chopped

Servings: 4
Cooking Time: 30 minutes

Directions:

1. Start by preheating your Air Fryer to 370 degrees F.
2. Drizzle the avocado oil all over the chicken breast. Then, rub the chicken breast with the Jamaican Jerk rub.
3. Cook in the preheated Air Fryer approximately 15 minutes. Turn them over and cook an additional 8 minutes.
4. While the chicken breasts are roasting, combine the salt, agave syrup, and mustard in a pan over medium heat. Let it simmer until the glaze thickens.
5. After that, brush the glaze all over the chicken breast. Air-fry for a further 6 minutes or until the surface is crispy. Serve garnished with fresh scallions. Bon appétit!

Herbed Roasted Chicken

Ingredients:

- 1 (5-pounds) whole chicken
- 3 garlic cloves, minced
- 1 teaspoon fresh lemon zest, finely grated
- 1 teaspoon dried thyme, crushed
- 1 teaspoon dried oregano, crushed
- 1 teaspoon dried rosemary, crushed
- 1 teaspoon smoked paprika
- Salt and ground black pepper, as required
- 2 tablespoons fresh lemon juice
- 2 tablespoons olive oil

Servings: 7
Cooking Time: 1 hour

Directions:

1. Preheat the Air fryer to 360 o F and grease an Air fryer basket.
2. Mix the garlic, lemon zest, herbs and spices in a bowl.
3. Rub the herb mixture over the chicken and drizzle with lemon juice and oil.
4. Keep aside for about 2 hours at room temperature and transfer into the Air fryer.
5. Cook for about 50 minutes and carefully flip the chicken.
6. Cook for 10 more minutes and dish out in a plate.
7. Cut into desired size pieces with a knife and serve warm.

Snacks & Appetizers Recipes

French Fries

Ingredients:

- 1 lb. russet potatoes
- 1 tsp. salt
- ½ tsp. black pepper
- 1 tbsp. olive oil

Servings: 4
Cooking Time: 25 minutes

Directions:

1. In a pot filled with water, blanch the potatoes until softened.
2. Remove from the heat and allow to cool. Slice the potatoes into matchstick shapes.
3. Place them in a large bowl and coat with the olive oil, salt and pepper.
4. Pre-heat the Air Fryer to 390°F.
5. Cook the French fries for about 15 minutes, giving the basket a shake now and again throughout the cooking time. Serve with freshly chopped herbs if desired.

Green Bean Crisps

Ingredients:

- 1 egg, beaten
- 1/4 cup cornmeal
- 1/4 cup parmesan, grated
- 1 teaspoon sea salt
- 1/2 teaspoon red pepper flakes, crushed
- 1 pound green beans
- 2 tablespoons grapeseed oil

Servings: 4
Cooking Time: 20 minutes

Directions:

1. In a mixing bowl, combine together the egg, cornmeal, parmesan, salt, and red pepper flakes; mix to combine well.
2. Dip the green beans into the batter and transfer them to the cooking basket. Brush with the grapeseed oil.
3. Cook in the preheated Air Fryer at 390 degrees F for 4 minutes. Shake the basket and cook for a further 3 minutes. Work in batches.
4. Taste, adjust the seasonings and serve. Bon appétit!

Dad's Boozy Wings

Servings: 4
Cooking Time:
1 hour 15 minutes

Ingredients:

- 2 teaspoons coriander seeds
- 1 ½ tablespoons soy sauce
- 1/3 cup vermouth
- 3/4 pound chicken wings
- 1 ½ tablespoons each fish sauce
- 2 tablespoons melted butter
- 1 teaspoon seasoned salt
- Freshly ground black pepper, to taste

Directions:

1. Rub the chicken wings with the black pepper and seasoned salt; now, add the other ingredients.
2. Next, soak the chicken wings in this mixture for 55 minutes in the refrigerator.
3. Air-fry the chicken wings at 365 degrees F for 16 minutes or until warmed through. Bon appétit!

Chicken Nuggets

Servings: 4
Cooking Time: 10 minutes

Ingredients:

- 20-ounce chicken breast, cut into chunks
- 1 cup all-purpose flour
- 2 tablespoons milk
- 1 egg
- 1 cup panko breadcrumbs
- ½ tablespoon mustard powder
- 1 tablespoon garlic powder
- 1 tablespoon onion powder
- Salt and black pepper, to taste

Directions:

1. Preheat the Air fryer to 390 o F and grease an Air fryer basket.
2. Put chicken along with mustard powder, garlic powder, onion powder, salt and black pepper in a food processor and pulse until combined.
3. Place flour in a shallow dish and whisk the eggs with milk in a second dish.
4. Place breadcrumbs in a third shallow dish.
5. Coat the nuggets evenly in flour and dip in the egg mixture.
6. Roll into the breadcrumbs evenly and arrange the nuggets in an Air fryer basket.
7. Cook for about 10 minutes and dish out to serve warm.

Cheese Pastries

**Servings: 6
Cooking Time: 5 minutes**

Ingredients:

- 1 egg yolk
- 4 ounces feta cheese, crumbled
- 1 scallion, finely chopped
- 2 tablespoons fresh parsley, finely chopped
- Salt and ground black pepper, as needed
- 2 frozen filo pastry sheets, thawed
- 2 tablespoons olive oil

Directions:

1. In a large bowl, add the egg yolk, and beat well.
2. Add in the feta cheese, scallion, parsley, salt, and black pepper. Mix well.
3. Cut each filo pastry sheet in three strips.
4. Add about 1 teaspoon of feta mixture on the underside of a strip.
5. Fold the tip of sheet over the filling in a zigzag manner to form a triangle.
6. Repeat with the remaining strips and fillings.
7. Set the temperature of Air Fryer to 390 degrees F.
8. Coat each pastry evenly with oil.
9. Place the pastries in an Air Fryer basket in a single layer.
10. Air Fry for about 3 minutes, then air fryer for about 2 minutes on 360 degrees F.
11. Serve.

Cashew Dip

Ingredients:
- ½ cup cashews, soaked in water for 4 hours and drained
- 3 tablespoons cilantro, chopped
- 2 garlic cloves, minced
- 1 teaspoon lime juice
- A pinch of salt and black pepper
- 2 tablespoons coconut milk

Servings: 6
Cooking Time: 8 minutes

Directions:
1. In a blender, combine all the ingredients, pulse well and transfer to a ramekin. Put the ramekin in your air fryer's basket and cook at 350 degrees F for 8 minutes. Serve as a party dip.

Broccoli Florets

Ingredients:
- 1 lb. broccoli, cut into florets
- 1 tbsp. lemon juice
- 1 tbsp. olive oil
- 1 tbsp. sesame seeds
- 3 garlic cloves, minced

Servings: 4
Cooking Time: 20 minutes

Directions:
1. In a bowl, combine all of the ingredients, coating the broccoli well.
2. Transfer to the Air Fryer basket and air fry at 400°F for 13 minutes.

BBQ Lil Smokies

Ingredients:
- 1 pound beef cocktail wieners
- 10 ounces barbecue sauce, no sugar added

Servings: 6
Cooking Time: 20 minutes

Directions:
1. Start by preheating your Air Fryer to 380 degrees F.
2. Prick holes into your sausages using a fork and transfer them to the baking pan.
3. Cook for 13 minutes. Spoon the barbecue sauce into the pan and cook an additional 2 minutes.
4. Serve with toothpicks. Bon appétit!

Bacon-Wrapped Shrimp

Ingredients:
- 1 pound bacon, sliced thinly
- 1 pound shrimp, peeled and deveined
- Salt, to taste

Servings: 6
Cooking Time: 7 minutes

Directions:
1. Preheat the Air fryer to 390 o F and grease an Air fryer basket.
2. Wrap 1 shrimp with a bacon slices, covering completely.
3. Repeat with the remaining shrimp and bacon slices.
4. Arrange the bacon wrapped shrimps in a baking dish and freeze for about 15 minutes.
5. Place the shrimps in an Air fryer basket and cook for about 7 minutes.
6. Dish out and serve warm.

Hummus Mushroom Pizza

Servings: 4
Cooking Time: 6 minutes

Ingredients:

- 4 Portobello mushroom caps, stemmed and gills removed
- 3 ounces zucchini, shredded
- 2 tablespoons sweet red pepper, seeded and chopped
- 4 Kalamata olives, sliced
- ½ cup hummus
- 1 tablespoon balsamic vinegar
- Salt and black pepper, to taste
- 4 tablespoons pasta sauce
- 1 garlic clove, minced
- 1 teaspoon dried basil

Directions:

1. Preheat the Air fryer to 330 o F and grease an Air fryer basket.
2. Coat both sides of all Portobello mushroom cap with vinegar.
3. Season the inside of each mushroom cap with salt and black pepper.
4. Divide pasta sauce and garlic inside each mushroom.
5. Arrange mushroom caps into the Air fryer basket and cook for about 3 minutes.
6. Remove from the Air fryer and top zucchini, red peppers and olives on each mushroom cap.
7. Season with basil, salt, and black pepper and transfer into the Air fryer basket.
8. Cook for about 3 more minutes and dish out in a serving platter.
9. Spread hummus on each mushroom pizza and serve.

Bacon and Onion Fat Bombs

Ingredients:

- 2 onions, sliced
- 1 cup bacon, finely chopped
- 1/2 cup Colby cheese, shredded
- 8 ounces soft cheese
- 2 ½ tablespoons canola oil
- 2 eggs

Servings: 6
Cooking Time: 15 minutes

Directions:

1. Combine all the ingredients in a mixing dish. Roll the mixture into bite-sized balls.
2. Air-fry them at 390 degrees F for 5 minutes. Work in batches.
3. Serve with toothpicks and enjoy!

Lime Tomato Salsa

Ingredients:

- 4 tomatoes, cubed
- 3 chili peppers, minced
- 2 spring onions, chopped
- 1 garlic clove, minced
- 2 tablespoons lime juice
- 2 teaspoons cilantro, chopped
- 2 teaspoons parsley, chopped
- Cooking spray

Servings: 4
Cooking Time: 8 minutes

Directions:

1. Grease a pan that fits your air fryer with the cooking spray, and mix all the ingredients inside. Introduce the pan in the machine and cook at 360 degrees F for 8 minutes. Divide into bowls and serve as an appetizer.

Party Chicken Pillows

Servings: 4
Cooking Time: 20 minutes

Ingredients:

- 1 teaspoon olive oil
- 1 cup ground chicken
- 1 (8-ounces) can Pillsbury Crescent Roll dough
- Sea salt and ground black pepper, to taste
- 1 teaspoon onion powder
- 1/2 teaspoon garlic powder
- 4 tablespoons tomato paste
- 4 ounces cream cheese, at room temperature
- 2 tablespoons butter, melted

Directions:

1. Heat the olive oil in a pan over medium-high heat. Then, cook the ground chicken until browned or about 4 minutes.
2. Unroll the crescent dough. Roll out the dough using a rolling pin; cut into 8 pieces.
3. Place the browned chicken, salt, black pepper, onion powder, garlic powder, tomato paste, and cheese in the center of each piece.
4. Fold each corner over the filling using wet hands. Press together to cover the filling entirely and seal the edges.
5. Now, spritz the bottom of the Air Fryer basket with cooking oil. Lay the chicken pillows in a single layer in the cooking basket. Drizzle the melted butter all over chicken pillows.
6. Bake at 370 degrees F for 6 minutes or until golden brown. Work in batches. Bon appétit!

Almond Coconut Granola

Ingredients:

- 1 teaspoon monk fruit
- 1 teaspoon almond butter
- 1 teaspoon coconut oil
- 2 tablespoons almonds, chopped
- 1 teaspoon pumpkin puree
- ½ teaspoon pumpkin pie spices
- 2 tablespoons coconut flakes
- 2 tablespoons pumpkin seeds, crushed
- 1 teaspoon hemp seeds
- 1 teaspoon flax seeds
- Cooking spray

Servings: 4
Cooking Time: 12 minutes

Directions:

1. In the big bowl mix up almond butter and coconut oil. Microwave the mixture until it is melted. After this, in the separated bowl mix up monk fruit, pumpkin spices, coconut flakes, pumpkin seeds, hemp seeds, and flax seeds. Add the melted coconut oil and pumpkin puree. Then stir the mixture until it is homogenous.
2. Preheat the air fryer to 350F. Then put the pumpkin mixture on the baking paper and make the shape of the square. After this, cut the square on the serving bars and transfer in the preheated air fryer. Cook the pumpkin granola for 12 minutes.

Portabella Pizza Treat

Servings: 2
Cooking Time: 6 minutes

Ingredients:

- 2 Portabella caps, stemmed
- 2 tablespoons canned tomatoes with basil
- 2 tablespoons mozzarella cheese, shredded
- 4 pepperoni slices
- 2 tablespoons Parmesan cheese, grated freshly
- 2 tablespoon olive oil
- 1/8 teaspoon dried Italian seasonings
- Salt, to taste
- 1 teaspoon red pepper flakes, crushed

Directions:

1. Preheat the Air fryer to 320 o F and grease an Air fryer basket.
2. Drizzle olive oil on both sides of portabella cap and season salt, red pepper flakes and Italian seasonings.
3. Top canned tomatoes on the mushrooms, followed by mozzarella cheese.
4. Place portabella caps in the Air fryer basket and cook for about 2 minutes.
5. Top with pepperoni slices and cook for about 4 minutes.
6. Sprinkle with Parmesan cheese and dish out to serve warm.

Fish & Seafood Recipes

Creamy Crab Dip

Ingredients:

- 1/2 cup crabmeat, cooked
- 1/2 tsp pepper
- 1 tbsp hot sauce
- 1/4 cup scallions
- 1 cup cheese, grated
- 1 tbsp mayonnaise
- 1 tbsp parsley, chopped
- 1 tbsp lemon juice
- 1/4 tsp salt

Servings: 2
Cooking Time: 7 minutes

Directions:

1. In an air fryer baking dish, mix together crabmeat, hot sauce, scallions, cheese, mayonnaise, pepper, and salt.
2. Place dish into the air fryer basket and cook at 400 F for 7 minutes.
3. Add parsley and lemon juice. Stir well.
4. Serve and enjoy.

Fijan Coconut Fish

Servings: 2
Cooking Time: 20 minutes

Ingredients:

- 1 cup coconut milk
- 2 tablespoons lime juice
- 2 tablespoons Shoyu sauce
- Salt and white pepper, to taste
- 1 teaspoon turmeric powder
- 1/2 teaspoon ginger powder
- 1/2 Thai Bird's Eye chili, seeded and finely chopped
- 1 pound tilapia
- 2 tablespoons olive oil

Directions:

1. In a mixing bowl, thoroughly combine the coconut milk with the lime juice, Shoyu sauce, salt, pepper, turmeric, ginger, and chili pepper. Add tilapia and let it marinate for 1 hour.
2. Brush the Air Fryer basket with olive oil. Discard the marinade and place the tilapia fillets in the Air Fryer basket.
3. Cook the tilapia in the preheated Air Fryer at 400 degrees F for 6 minutes; turn them over and cook for 6 minutes more. Work in batches.
4. Serve with some extra lime wedges if desired. Enjoy!

Cod with Asparagus

Ingredients:

- 2 (6-ounces) boneless cod fillets
- 2 tablespoons fresh parsley, roughly chopped
- 2 tablespoons fresh dill, roughly chopped
- 1 bunch asparagus
- 1½ tablespoons fresh lemon juice
- 1 tablespoon olive oil
- Salt and black pepper, to taste

Directions:

1. Preheat the Air fryer to 400 o F and grease an Air fryer basket.
2. Mix lemon juice, oil, herbs, salt, and black pepper in a small bowl.
3. Combine the cod and ¾ of the oil mixture in another bowl.
4. Coat asparagus with remaining oil mixture and transfer to the Air fryer basket.
5. Cook for about 3 minutes and arrange cod fillets on top of asparagus.
6. Cook for about 8 minutes and dish out in serving plates.

Servings: 2
Cooking Time: 11 minutes

Coconut Prawns

Servings: 4
Cooking Time: 10 minutes

Ingredients:

- 12 prawns, cleaned and deveined
- Salt and ground black pepper, to taste
- ½ tsp. cumin powder
- 1 tsp. fresh lemon juice
- 1 medium egg, whisked
- ⅓ cup of beer
- ½ cup flour
- 1 tsp. baking powder
- 1 tbsp. curry powder
- ½ tsp. grated fresh ginger
- 1 cup flaked coconut

Directions:

1. Coat the prawns in the salt, pepper, cumin powder, and lemon juice.
2. In a bowl, combine together the whisked egg, beer, a quarter-cup of the flour, baking powder, curry, and ginger.
3. In a second bowl, put the remaining quarter-cup of flour, and in a third bowl, the flaked coconut.
4. Dredge the prawns in the flour, before coating them in the beer mixture. Finally, coat your prawns in the flaked coconut.
5. Air-fry at 360°F for 5 minutes. Flip them and allow to cook on the other side for another 2 to 3 minutes before serving.

Chunky Fish

Servings: 4
Cooking Time: 10 minutes

Ingredients:

- 2 cans canned fish
- 2 celery stalks, trimmed and finely chopped
- 1 egg, whisked
- 1 cup friendly bread crumbs
- 1 tsp. whole-grain mustard
- ½ tsp. sea salt
- ¼ tsp. freshly cracked black peppercorns
- 1 tsp. paprika

Directions:

1. Combine all of the ingredients in the order in which they appear. Mold the mixture into four equal-sized cakes. Leave to chill in the refrigerator for 50 minutes.
2. Put on an Air Fryer grill pan. Spritz all sides of each cake with cooking spray.
3. Grill at 360°F for 5 minutes. Turn the cakes over and resume cooking for an additional 3 minutes.
4. Serve with mashed potatoes if desired.

Cheesy Lemon Halibut

Ingredients:

- 1 lb. halibut fillet
- ½ cup butter
- 2 ½ tbsp. mayonnaise
- 2 ½ tbsp. lemon juice
- ¾ cup parmesan cheese, grated

Servings: 2
Cooking Time: 20 minutes

Directions:

1. Pre-heat your fryer at 375°F.
2. Spritz the halibut fillets with cooking spray and season as desired.
3. Put the halibut in the fryer and cook for twelve minutes.
4. In the meantime, combine the butter, mayonnaise, and lemon juice in a bowl with a hand mixer. Ensure a creamy texture is achieved.
5. Stir in the grated parmesan.
6. When the halibut is ready, open the drawer and spread the butter over the fish with a butter knife. Allow to cook for a further two minutes, then serve hot.

Cajun Spiced Salmon

Ingredients:
- 2 (7-ounces) (¾-inch thick) salmon fillets
- 1 tablespoon Cajun seasoning
- ½ teaspoon sugar
- 1 tablespoon fresh lemon juice

Servings: 2
Cooking Time: 8 minutes

Directions:
1. Preheat the Air fryer to 365 o F and grease an Air fryer grill pan.
2. Season the salmon evenly with Cajun seasoning and sugar.
3. Arrange the salmon fillets into the Air fryer grill pan, skin-side up.
4. Cook for about 8 minutes and dish out the salmon fillets in the serving plates.
5. Drizzle with the lemon juice and serve hot.

Buttered Scallops

Ingredients:
- ¾ pound sea scallops, cleaned and patted very dry
- 1 tablespoon butter, melted
- ½ tablespoon fresh thyme, minced
- Salt and black pepper, as required

Servings: 2
Cooking Time: 4 minutes

Directions:
1. Preheat the Air fryer to 390 o F and grease an Air fryer basket.
2. Mix scallops, butter, thyme, salt, and black pepper in a bowl.
3. Arrange scallops in the Air fryer basket and cook for about 4 minutes.
4. Dish out the scallops in a platter and serve hot.

Fried Crawfish

Ingredients:

- 1-pound crawfish
- 1 tablespoon avocado oil
- 1 teaspoon onion powder
- 1 tablespoon rosemary, chopped

Servings: 4
Cooking Time: 5 minutes

Directions:

1. Preheat the air fryer to 340F. Place the crawfish in the air fryer basket and sprinkle with avocado oil and rosemary. Add the onion powder and stir the crawfish gently. Cook the meal for 5 minutes.

Breadcrumbed Fish

Ingredients:

- 4 tbsp. vegetable oil
- 5 oz. friendly bread crumbs
- 1 egg
- 4 medium fish fillets

Servings: 2-4
Cooking Time: 25 minutes

Directions:

1. Pre-heat your Air Fryer to 350°F.
2. In a bowl, combine the bread crumbs and oil.
3. In a separate bowl, stir the egg with a whisk. Dredge each fish fillet in the egg before coating it in the crumbs mixture. Put them in Air Fryer basket.
4. Cook for 12 minutes and serve hot.

Garlicky Grilled Shrimp

Ingredients:

- 18 shrimps, shelled and deveined
- 2 tablespoons freshly squeezed lemon juice
- 1/2 teaspoon hot paprika
- 1/2 teaspoon salt
- 1 teaspoon lemon-pepper seasoning
- 2 tablespoons extra-virgin olive oil
- 2 garlic cloves, peeled and minced
- 1 teaspoon onion powder
- 1/4 teaspoon cumin powder
- 1/2 cup fresh parsley, coarsely chopped

Servings: 4
Cooking Time: 35 minutes

Directions:

1. Place all the ingredients in a mixing dish; gently stir, cover and let it marinate for 30 minutes in the refrigerator.
2. Air-fry in the preheated Air Fryer at 400 degrees F for 5 minutes or until the shrimps turn pink. Bon appétit!

Baked Cod

Servings: 4
Cooking Time: 12 minutes

Ingredients:

- 4 cod fillets, boneless
- Salt and black pepper to taste
- 2 tablespoons parsley, chopped
- A drizzle of olive oil
- ¾ teaspoon sweet paprika
- ½ teaspoon oregano, dried
- ½ teaspoon thyme, dried
- ½ teaspoon basil, dried
- Juice of 1 lemon
- 2 tablespoons butter, melted

Directions:

1. Add all ingredients to a bowl and toss gently.
2. Transfer the fish to your air fryer and cook at 380 degrees F for 6 minutes on each side.
3. Serve right away.

Herbed Haddock

Servings: 2
Cooking Time: 8 minutes

Ingredients:

- 2 (6-ounce) haddock fillets
- 2 tablespoons pine nuts
- 3 tablespoons fresh basil, chopped
- 1 tablespoon Parmesan cheese, grated
- ½ cup extra-virgin olive oil
- Salt and black pepper, to taste

Directions:

1. Preheat the Air fryer to 355 o F and grease an Air fryer basket.
2. Coat the haddock fillets evenly with olive oil and season with salt and black pepper.
3. Place the haddock fillets in the Air fryer basket and cook for about 8 minutes.
4. Dish out the haddock fillets in serving plates.
5. Meanwhile, put remaining ingredients in a food processor and pulse until smooth.
6. Top this cheese sauce over the haddock fillets and serve hot.

Almond Coconut Shrimp

Servings: 4
Cooking Time: 5 minutes

Ingredients:

- 16 oz shrimp, peeled
- 1/2 cup almond flour
- 2 egg whites
- 1/4 tsp cayenne pepper
- 1/2 cup unsweetened shredded coconut
- 1/2 tsp salt

Directions:

1. Preheat the air fryer to 400 F.
2. Spray air fryer basket with cooking spray.
3. Whisk egg whites in a shallow dish.
4. In a bowl, mix together the shredded coconut, almond flour, and cayenne pepper.
5. Dip shrimp into the egg mixture then coat with coconut mixture.
6. Place coated shrimp into the air fryer basket and cook for 5 minutes.
7. Serve and enjoy.

Italian Shrimp Scampi

Ingredients:

- 2 egg whites
- 1/2 cup coconut flour
- 1 cup Parmigiano-Reggiano, grated
- 1/2 teaspoon celery seeds
- 1/2 teaspoon porcini powder
- 1/2 teaspoon onion powder
- 1 teaspoon garlic powder
- 1/2 teaspoon dried rosemary
- 1/2 teaspoon sea salt
- 1/2 teaspoon ground black pepper
- 1 ½ pounds shrimp, deveined

Servings: 4
Cooking Time: 20 minutes

Directions:

1. Whisk the egg with coconut flour and Parmigiano-Reggiano. Add in seasonings and mix to combine well.
2. Dip your shrimp in the batter. Roll until they are covered on all sides.
3. Cook in the preheated Air Fryer at 390 degrees F for 5 to 7 minutes or until golden brown. Work in batches. Serve with lemon wedges if desired.

Vegetable & Side Dishes Recipes

Indian Red Potatoes

Servings: 5
Cooking Time: 20 minutes

Ingredients:

- 2 pounds red potatoes, cubed
- ½ teaspoon mustard seeds
- 1 teaspoon garlic, minced
- ¼ cup veggie stock
- ½ cup mint
- ½ cup cilantro
- 1 teaspoon ginger, grated
- 2 teaspoons lime juice
- Salt and black pepper to taste

Directions:

1. In a blender, add the stock, mint, cilantro, ginger, lime juice, salt, and pepper; pulse well.
2. Then place this mint mix into a pan that fits your air fryer, along with the remaining ingredients, and toss.
3. Place the pan in the fryer and cook at 370 degrees F for 20 minutes.
4. Divide the potatoes between plates and serve as a side dish.

Garlic Broccoli Rabe

Ingredients:

- 7 oz broccoli rabe, roughly chopped
- 2 tablespoons almond flour
- 1 teaspoon coconut oil, melted
- ¼ teaspoon salt
- 1 tablespoon avocado oil
- 1 teaspoon garlic powder

Servings: 4
Cooking Time: 20 minutes

Directions:

1. Preheat the air fryer to 355F. In the mixing bowl, mix up broccoli rabe, salt, garlic powder, and melted coconut oil. Mix up the greens and sprinkle them with almond flour. Shake them well.
2. After this, sprinkle the broccoli rabe with avocado oil and transfer in the air fryer. Cook the greens for 20 minutes. Shake them every 5 minutes to avoid burning.

Famous Fried Pickles

Ingredients:

- 1/3 cup milk
- 1 teaspoon garlic powder
- 2 medium-sized eggs
- 1 teaspoon fine sea salt
- 1/3 teaspoon chili powder
- 1/3 cup all-purpose flour
- 1/2 teaspoon shallot powder
- 2 jars sweet and sour pickle spears

Servings: 6
Cooking Time: 20 minutes

Directions:

1. Pat the pickle spears dry with a kitchen towel. Then, take two mixing bowls.
2. Whisk the egg and milk in a bowl. In another bowl, combine all dry ingredients.
3. Firstly, dip the pickle spears into the dry mix; then coat each pickle with the egg/milk mixture; dredge them in the flour mixture again for additional coating.
4. Air fry battered pickles for 15 minutes at 385 degrees. Enjoy!

Dill Tomato

Ingredients:
- 1 oz Parmesan, sliced
- 1 tomato
- 1 teaspoon fresh dill, chopped
- 1 teaspoon olive oil
- ¼ teaspoon dried thyme

Servings: 2
Cooking Time: 8 minutes

Directions:
1. Trim the tomato and slice it on 2 pieces. Then preheat the air fryer to 350F. Top the tomato slices with sliced Parmesan, chopped fresh dill, and thyme. Sprinkle the tomatoes with olive oil and put in the air fryer.
2. Cook the meal for 8 minutes. Remove cooked tomato parm from the air fryer with the help of the spatula.

Chives Endives

Ingredients:
- 4 endives, trimmed
- A pinch of salt and black pepper
- ¼ cup goat cheese, crumbled
- 1 teaspoon lemon zest, grated
- 1 tablespoon lemon juice
- 2 tablespoons chives, chopped
- 2 tablespoons olive oil

Servings: 4
Cooking Time: 15 minutes

Directions:
1. In a bowl, mix the endives with the other ingredients except the cheese and chives and toss well. Put the endives in your air fryer's basket and cook at 380 degrees F for 15 minutes. Divide the corn between plates and serve with cheese and chives sprinkled on top.

Cheese Lings

Ingredients:
- 1 cup flour
- small cubes cheese, grated
- ¼ tsp. chili powder
- 1 tsp. butter
- Salt to taste
- 1 tsp. baking powder

Servings: 6
Cooking Time: 25 minutes

Directions:
1. Combine all the ingredients to form a dough, along with a small amount water as necessary.
2. Divide the dough into equal portions and roll each one into a ball.
3. Pre-heat Air Fryer at 360°F.
4. Transfer the balls to the fryer and air fry for 5 minutes, stirring periodically.

Butter Endives

Ingredients:
- 4 endives, trimmed and halved
- Salt and black pepper to taste
- 1 tablespoon lime juice
- 1 tablespoon butter, melted

Servings: 4
Cooking Time: 10 minutes

Directions:
1. Put the endives in your air fryer, and add the salt, pepper, lemon juice, and butter.
2. Cook at 360 degrees F for 10 minutes.
3. Divide between plates and serve.

Best Roasted Broccoli

Ingredients:

- 2 cups broccoli florets
- 2 tablespoons yogurt
- 1 tablespoon chickpea flour
- ¼ teaspoons turmeric powder
- ½ teaspoon salt
- ¼ teaspoon chaat masala

Servings: 2
Cooking Time: 15 minutes

Directions:

1. Place all ingredients in a bowl and toss to combine.
2. Place the baking dish accessory into the air fryer and place the food into the dish.
3. Close the air fryer and cook for 15 minutes at 3500F.
4. Halfway through the cooking time, give the baking dish a good shake.

Lemon Asparagus

Ingredients:

- 1 pound asparagus, trimmed
- A pinch of salt and black pepper
- 2 tablespoons olive oil
- 3 garlic cloves, minced
- 3 tablespoons parmesan, grated
- Juice of 1 lemon

Servings: 4
Cooking Time: 12 minutes

Directions:

1. In a bowl, mix the asparagus with the rest of the ingredients and toss. Put the asparagus in your air fryer's basket and cook at 390 degrees F for 12 minutes. Divide between plates and serve.

Balsamic Cabbage Mix

Ingredients:

- 6 cups green cabbage, shredded
- 6 radishes, sliced
- ½ cup celery leaves, chopped
- ¼ cup green onions, chopped
- 2 tablespoons balsamic vinegar
- 1 teaspoon lemon juice
- 3 tablespoons olive oil
- ½ teaspoon hot paprika

Servings: 4
Cooking Time: 15 minutes

Directions:

1. In your air fryer's pan, combine all the ingredients and toss well.
2. Introduce the pan in the fryer and cook at 380 degrees F for 15 minutes. Divide between plates and serve as a side dish.

Cheese Zucchini Rolls

Ingredients:

- 1 large zucchini, trimmed
- 1 teaspoon keto tomato sauce
- 3 oz Mozzarella, sliced
- 1 teaspoon olive oil

Servings: 2
Cooking Time: 10 minutes

Directions:

1. Slice the zucchini on the long thin slices. Then sprinkle every zucchini slice with marinara sauce and top with sliced Mozzarella. Roll the zucchini and secure it with toothpicks. Preheat the air fryer to 385F. Put the zucchini rolls in the air fryer and sprinkle them with olive oil. Cook the zucchini rolls for 10 minutes.

Mini Cheese Scones

Ingredients:

- Salt and pepper to taste
- ¾ oz butter
- 1 tsp chives
- 1 whole egg
- 1 tbsp milk
- 2 ¾ cheddar cheese, shredded

Servings: 10
Cooking Time: 25 minutes

Directions:

1. Preheat your air fryer to 340 F. In a bowl, mix butter, flour, cheddar cheese, chives, milk and egg to get a sticky dough. Dust a flat surface with flour. Roll the dough into small balls.
2. Place the balls in your air fryer's cooking basket and cook for 20 minutes. Serve and enjoy!

Asian Broccoli

Ingredients:

- 1 lb broccoli, cut into florets
- 1 tsp rice vinegar
- 2 tsp sriracha
- 2 tbsp soy sauce
- 1 tbsp garlic, minced
- 5 drops liquid stevia
- 1 1/2 tbsp sesame oil
- Salt

Servings: 4
Cooking Time: 20 minutes

Directions:

1. In a bowl, toss together broccoli, garlic, oil, and salt.
2. Spread broccoli in air fryer basket and cook for 15-20 minutes at 400 F.
3. Meanwhile, in a microwave-safe bowl mix together soy sauce, vinegar, liquid stevia, and sriracha and microwave for 10 seconds.
4. Transfer broccoli to a bowl and toss well with soy mixture to coat.
5. Serve and enjoy.

Parmesan Cherry Tomatoes

Ingredients:

- 1 tablespoon ghee, melted
- 2 cups cherry tomatoes, halved
- 3 tablespoons scallions, chopped
- 1 teaspoon lemon zest, grated
- 2 tablespoons parsley, chopped
- ¼ cup parmesan, grated

Servings: 4
Cooking Time: 15 minutes

Directions:

1. In a pan that fits the air fryer, combine all the ingredients except the parmesan, and toss. Sprinkle the parmesan on top, introduce the pan in the machine and cook at 360 degrees F for 10 minutes. Divide between plates and serve.

Pop Corn Broccoli

Ingredients:

- 4 egg yolks
- ¼ cup butter, melted
- 2 cups coconut flower
- Salt and pepper
- 2 cups broccoli florets

Servings: 1
Cooking Time: 10 minutes

Directions:

1. In a bowl, whisk the egg yolks and melted butter together. Throw in the coconut flour, salt and pepper, then stir again to combine well.
2. Pre-heat the fryer at 400°F.
3. Dip each broccoli floret into the mixture and place in the fryer. Cook for six minutes, in multiple batches if necessary. Take care when removing them from the fryer and enjoy!

Air Fried Vegetable Tempura

Servings: 3
Cooking Time: 20 minutes

Ingredients:

- 1 cup broccoli florets
- 1 red bell pepper, cut into strips
- 1 small sweet potato, peeled and cut into thick slices
- 1 small zucchini, cut into thick slices
- ⅔ cup cornstarch
- ⅓ cup all-purpose flour
- 1 egg, beaten
- ¾ cup club soda
- 1½ cups panko breadcrumbs
- Non-stick cooking spray

Directions:

1. Mix the cornstarch and all-purpose flour. Dredge the vegetables in this mixture.
2. Mix egg and club soda. Dip each flour-coated vegetable into this mixture soda before dredging in bread crumbs.
3. Place the vegetables on the double layer rack accessory and spray with cooking oil.
4. Place inside the air fryer.
5. Close and cook for 20 minutes at 3500F.